EPHESIANS 6:10-18

The Armor of God

D1599994

BIBLE CHAPTERS
FOR KIDS

I can be strong during difficult times, because I have God's power with me.

"Be strong in the Lord, and in the power of His might."

God's power is like a spiritual armor that protects me from the devil's temptations.

"Put on the whole armor of God, so that you can stand strong against the devil's plans."

I should not fight against others that might do mean things to me, but rather against the evil and the bad.

"We don't fight against people on earth, but against the devil's kingdom."

The devil is our enemy,
but we can't see him or
strike at him physically.

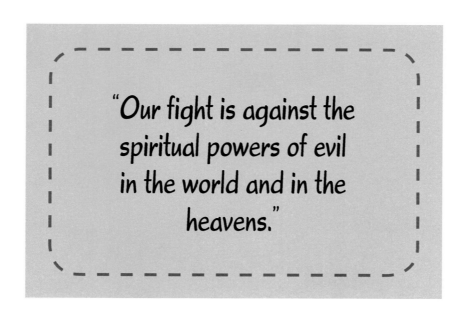

"Our fight is against the
spiritual powers of evil
in the world and in the
heavens."

I have to get myself ready.
Like a great warrior of God,
I can learn how to put on a
spiritual armor to protect me.

"That's why we need to put on
the whole armor of God, so that
we may be able to stand strong
when evil comes our way."

The belt worn by a Roman soldier was important, because it kept together his whole suit. It also held the weapons he needed to fight with.

God is strong and powerful, and He is always with me. Like a good tight belt, the truth of God's Word will support and protect me.

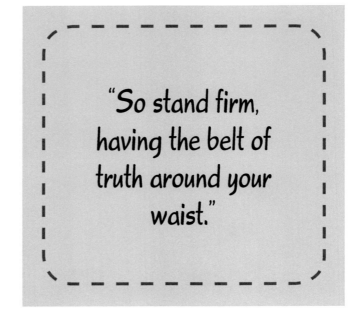

"So stand firm, having the belt of truth around your waist."

God teaches me to do what is right and to show kindness, even when the devil tries to pull me the other way. I guard my own heart and demonstrate that I'm strong with God's help by showing love to others.

"And on your chest, wear the breastplate of righteousness."

I am ready to go and tell others about the good news of God's love and peace.

Strong footwear was always important for a soldier who had to be prepared to travel far, and at a moment's notice.

"And on your feet, prepare yourself to walk and spread the good news of peace."

I use the shield of faith to protect myself from the devil! Faith is to trust God and believe in Him, even though I can't see Him with my eyes. God believes in me, and I believe in Him. When I trust in God, I am strong.

"By taking the shield of faith, you will be able to put out all the fiery darts of the wicked."

Jesus' sacrifice protects my soul in the same way that a helmet protects my head. God rescued me from my mistakes when Jesus died to save me.

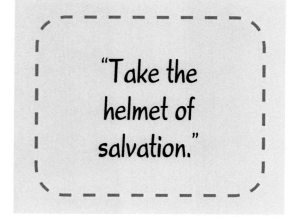

"Take the helmet of salvation."

I can use God's Word as a powerful weapon against the devil. When I'm tempted to do something wrong, the Bible reminds me of what I should do instead.

"And take the sword of the Spirit, which is the Word of God."

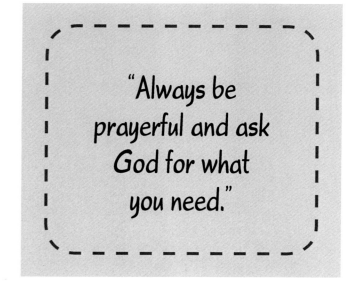

Now that I have my spiritual armor on, I will practice using it. I pray often and ask Jesus to guide me.

"Always be prayerful and ask God for what you need."

I need to be ready to face the devil at all times and pray that others can do so as well.

"You must always be ready and never give up. Pray often for all of God's people."

Dear God,

Please help me to put on Your armor of the spirit every day.

Help me to choose good when I am tempted to do wrong.

Teach me to

do the loving thing.

Give me boldness to tell others about You. Remind me to read and follow Your Word.

God, please make me strong in You. Amen.

a time to praise

Thank You, dear God,
that You have given me
this armor of protection
against the devil.

Thank You for giving
me strength, even when
I feel weak.

I praise You for always
being there to help me.

iCHARACTER

Published by iCharacter Ltd. (Ireland)
www.icharacter.org
By Agnes and Salem de Bezenac
Illustrated by Agnes de Bezenac
Colored by Henny
Copyright 2014. All rights reserved.
ISBN 978-1-62387-011-9
All Bible verses adapted from the KJV.

Made in the USA
Lexington, KY
12 December 2017